Lesley Riley

Creative Image Transfer

Any Artist · Any Style · Any Surface

16 New Mixed-Media Projects Using Transfer Artist Paper

Text copyright © 2014 by Lesley Riley

Photography and Artwork copyright © 2014 by C&T Publishing, Inc.

Publisher: **Amy Marson**

Creative Director: **Gailen Runge**

Art Director: **Kristy Zacharias**

Editor: **Lynn Koolish**

Technical Editor: **Helen Frost**

Cover Designer: **April Mostek**

Book Designer: **Rose Wright**

Production Coordinator: **Rue Flaherty**

Production Editor: **Katie Van Amburg**

Illustrator: **Rue Flaherty**

Photo Assistant: **Mary Peyton Peppo**

Photography by **Diane Pedersen**, unless otherwise noted

Published by C&T Publishing, Inc., P.O. Box 1456, Lafayette, CA 94549

Attention Teachers: C&T Publishing, Inc., encourages you to use this book as a text for teaching. Contact us at 800-284-1114 or www.ctpub.com for lesson plans and information about the C&T Creative Troupe.

Library of Congress

Riley, Lesley, 1952-

Creative image transfer--any artist, any style, any surface : 16 new mixed-media projects using TAP transfer artist paper / Lesley Riley.

pages cm

ISBN 978-1-60705-831-1 (soft cover)

1. Handicraft. 2. Transfer-printing. 3. Mixed media (Art) I. Title.

TT880.R555 2014

745.5--dc23   2013049475

Printed in China

10 9 8 7 6 5 4 3 2 1

Dedication

I live for art, but without family, I live for naught.
To my ever-growing, ever-loving ever sources of inspiration
and encouragement: Buddy, Brian, Amy, Emma,
Annie, Kathryn, Sara, Jeff, Julia, Jillian, Chris, Jena,
Samantha, Marc, Riley, Reese, Kerry, Kelly, Dad, Katie, Joe.
And to my mother, June, watching us all from above.

Acknowledgments

My name is on the cover, but a book is created
by many people. First, I give thanks to the artists
who answered my call and contributed their time
and art to enrich these pages.

A forever thank-you to Amy Marson and
everyone at C&T for giving the nod of approval to
another book. Thanks to Lynn Koolish for keeping
me on track and helping me translate creative acts
into understandable directions, along with Helen Frost,
Katie Van Amburg, and Rue Flaherty. Words in a craft
book are nothing without photographs and beautiful
pages. Kudos to the photography team, Diane Pedersen
and Mary Peyton Peppo, and book designer,
Rose Wright, for bringing my vision to life.

Contents

Introduction

While working on a project I jot down ideas on sticky notes—lots of sticky notes. While rummaging through them to be sure I didn't miss anything I wanted to put in this book, I came across these words that I wrote: "Art is our way to be everlasting." That we can create something of beauty, of meaning, of memory or sentiment is a wondrous thing. Through art we make our mark and leave something of ourselves behind, like a photograph passed down through generations.

I have always been in love with images, and now, today, most people have cameras at their fingertips and the ability to add filters and create striking effects without any experience at all. This has become a way of recording our lives, one moment at a time.

Author and photographer Jan Phillips says, "Photos are our autobiography, a way of telling who we are."

What are we to do with all of these photographs, these captured memories, marvels, and objects of desire? As Martin Parr says, "There are two parts to the process: taking the picture and finding ways of using it."

I have the perfect solution. TAP* those photos! TAP easily enables you to create a mixed bag—from craft to fine art. With TAP you can put a photo on a variety of surfaces, further opening up the possibilities of what you can create.

And TAP magic doesn't stop with photos! You can create your own artwork on TAP and transfer it, or scan your original art and transfer it onto a range of surfaces.

I am pleased, proud, and tickled pink to bring you another dose of TAP inspiration. I hope that you find a spark of an idea (or two, ten, or twenty!) within these pages and that you run with it. This book is full of wonderful creations presented to you as complete projects or jumping-off points and idea generators for your own work. Enough talk … let's get TAPping!

Lesley Riley's TAP Transfer Artist Paper (by C&T Publishing)—referred to as TAP throughout the chapter

The 4 W's of TAP

Lesley Riley's TAP Transfer Artist Paper (by C&T Publishing)
is referred to as TAP throughout the chapter.

TAP *(n)* an abbreviation for Lesley Riley's TAP Transfer Artist Paper. *I just got a new package of TAP. (v)* to transfer an image or artwork using Lesley Riley's TAP Transfer Artist Paper. *Mary TAPped a photo of her dog onto the canvas.*

I have been transferring images since the 1970s. Since then, I have taught a variety of transfer methods all over the world. As a result, I became known as the Transfer Queen in some circles. In December 2008, I made the decision and took the leap to introduce TAP to artists and crafters. Little did I know that in just a few years, people from Norway to South Africa, from the UK to New Zealand, and all across the United States would be creating with TAP—or as I like to say, TAPping.

In 2011 TAP won the Most Innovative New Product award at the Craft and Hobby Association (CHA) show. The judges were wowed by the variety of surfaces and the endless projects, from fine art to everyday crafts, that can be created with TAP.

Inspired by the first TAP book, *Create with TAP Transfer Artist Paper*, users have applied their own creativity and ingenuity to the product and created amazing works of art, gifts, memory quilts, journal pages, and more. It's time to take a second look at what TAP—and you—can do.

What Is TAP and How Does It Work?

I'm so glad you asked! TAP is a special type of paper that is spray-coated with a layer of polymer, a type of plastic. The coating accepts both the ink from your inkjet printer and a variety of art materials, allowing you to print or create your own artwork for transfer onto other surfaces.

When the paper is heated with an iron, the polymer fuses together with the art materials that have been applied to the surface and adheres to make a permanent, durable, and accurate transfer onto the surface of your choice.

It's almost as easy as it sounds. *Almost*, because there are a few things you need to know about transferring onto the range of surfaces you can TAP on. This book will give you all the basics you need to be successful. For the most in-depth discussion of the pros and cons of each surface, you may want to check out *Create with TAP Transfer Artist Paper*. It's available to you *(right now!)* as an eBook from www.ctpub.com as well as a hands-on paperback. It also includes fifteen different projects to inspire and ignite your creativity.

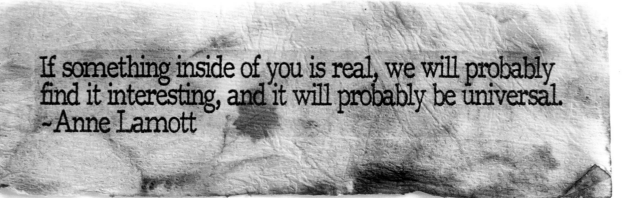

If something inside of you is real, we will probably find it interesting, and it will probably be universal.
~Anne Lamott

Why TAP? Why Not Just Paint, Draw, or Glue onto the Surface?

That's a great question and one I ask myself regularly.

Some of My Reasons for Using TAP

- I can't always paint as neatly or exactly as I would like, so I choose to TAP my images.

- Writing or painting words on different surfaces is exacting and tiring. TAPping text with standard or fancy fonts is easy.

- Glue can dry out and yellow. Glued paper can tear, come off, or get worn off. A TAPped image is permanent.

- TAP saves time. TAP transferring is much faster than direct painting or drawing.

- I can use my original art on a variety of surfaces.

- Different surfaces require different paints and preparation for surface design. TAP requires only an iron.

- You can wash and iron TAP transfers—they're permanent and won't fade on fabric.

Some Happy TAPpers' Reasons

LYNN KRAWCZYK I like to use markers with TAP. Markers often have bleed lines when you draw directly on fabric. With TAP, the image stays crisp and neat.

BARBARA STONE I use it because I like to transfer onto fabric and for the fabric to still have a soft hand. I love the way it looks like it just becomes part of the fabric.

LISA CHIN I like that the color stays vibrant when using TAP. I also like that if I mess up coloring something onto the TAP, I don't have use it; I can start over and get exactly what I want!

FAYTHE CROSBY Well, the smart aleck in me wants to say, "Because I love to iron!"—but that's a big old lie. I like it because you can have the piece of artwork and have the freedom to use it on a variety of different surfaces and not be limited to just the one you would have if you drew, painted, or printed on a specific surface.

ROBBIE PORTER PAYNE I can play with images in the computer, trace, draw (and erase!). You can transfer on so many different media with TAP! You can't do that with other products. And you can iron over it—you can't do that with other iron-on products.

HEIDI RAND I use it for my photographs and mixed-media photo artwork. It's great to get images onto surfaces that I can't print directly on, such as wood. It's the best transfer method I've found—and I teach transfers, so I know transfers!

AMY WILSON CAVANESS I'm transferring photos to fabric for memory quilts, and I love stitching on it—no big holes as with other iron-on products. Plus, I love the softness combined with rich color.

CECILE WHATMAN I love it because I am creative and can't draw. I use it because photos capture a point in time, an emotion, a place. I teach with it because it is reliable and fairly easy for students to use. I use it in classes with people who want to create art but are terrified of starting. It is transformative.

NORMAJEAN BREVIK I love how I can work in many transparent layers with TAP.

We're all hooked on the magic of TAP transfers!

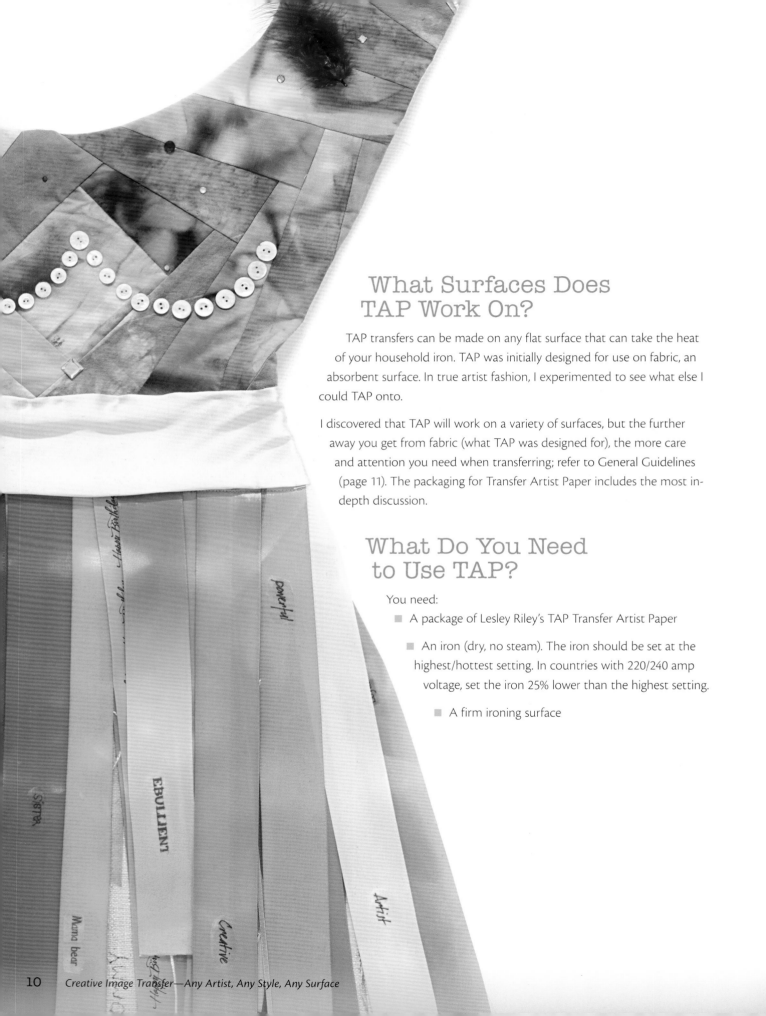

What Surfaces Does TAP Work On?

TAP transfers can be made on any flat surface that can take the heat of your household iron. TAP was initially designed for use on fabric, an absorbent surface. In true artist fashion, I experimented to see what else I could TAP onto.

I discovered that TAP will work on a variety of surfaces, but the further away you get from fabric (what TAP was designed for), the more care and attention you need when transferring; refer to General Guidelines (page 11). The packaging for Transfer Artist Paper includes the most in-depth discussion.

What Do You Need to Use TAP?

You need:

- A package of Lesley Riley's TAP Transfer Artist Paper

- An iron (dry, no steam). The iron should be set at the highest/hottest setting. In countries with 220/240 amp voltage, set the iron 25% lower than the highest setting.

- A firm ironing surface

TAP Transfer Basics

Lesley Riley's TAP Transfer Artist Paper (by C&T Publishing)
is referred to as TAP throughout the chapter.

Complete instructions are included with each
package of Lesley Riley's TAP Transfer Artist Paper.
Below are the basics to get you started.

Getting Your Images onto TAP

Get your art or images onto TAP in one (or more) of the following ways:

■ **PRINT**—Use an inkjet printer to print photos or scanned artwork or images on the white, coated side of TAP. No waiting or drying time is needed. *Important*—TAP cannot be used in a laser printer.

All transfers are a mirror image of the original unless you print your text and photos in reverse. Check your printer or photo-editing software for instructions on printing in reverse.

TAP Lesson

Fill Those TAP Sheets
Get the most from your TAP sheets by using photo-editing software to arrange as many images and/or words as will fit on each sheet.

■ **DRAW**—Any drawing materials can be used as long as you do not scratch the coating off the paper. Try markers, crayons, oil pastels, charcoal, and so on.

Areas where the polymer coating has been scratched off the paper will not transfer, but that's not always a bad thing. Keep this in mind as an optional technique when creating your art on TAP.

■ **PAINT**—Thin, watered-down layers of acrylic paints and full-strength or diluted acrylic or dye inks can be applied to TAP. Avoid thick applications of acrylic paint that will melt under the heat of the iron. Let the paint air-dry before ironing. Do not speed dry with a heat gun.

■ **USE MIXED MEDIA**—You can use rubber stamps, chalk pastels, spray inks, and more on TAP. The best way to answer the question "Will it work?" is to try it and see.

Ironing TAP to the Surface

General Guidelines

The following are general guidelines for ironing prepared TAP onto the surface of your choice. For more specific guidelines, see Specific Surface Guidelines (page 12).

■ For all areas of the image to transfer, the iron, TAP paper, and receiving surface must be in 100% contact. Gaps or bumps will cause areas where the image does not transfer completely.

■ Ensure that the ironing surface is firm, flat, and free of any threads or bumps.

■ Use a dry iron (no steam) preheated to the highest setting.* If your iron has an auto-shutoff feature, make sure it is hot when you are ready to transfer.

* For non-U.S. voltage (220/240), set your iron to 25% lower than the maximum setting.

- Use a low-tack tape such as blue painter's tape to prevent TAP paper from slipping on low- to nonabsorbent surfaces such as wood and metal.

- Keep your iron moving over the entire transfer area to ensure that it is uniformly hot.

- Always peel the TAP backing paper from the surface when hot. Peel back a corner (or two or three) to check that all areas have transferred to your liking. It's okay to iron incomplete areas again, but too much ironing may smear transfers not done on fabric. If the paper sticks while peeling, iron over it to reheat for release.

TAP Lesson

How Long to Iron

A good rule of thumb is to iron at least 7 seconds for every 5 square inches of transfer area except when noted. For example: 4″ × 6″ = about 7 seconds; 8″ × 10″ = about 14 seconds. Count your seconds "one thousand one, one thousand two…"

Specific Surface Guidelines

Fabric

All fabrics will work including cotton, silk, sheer, thin leather, burlap, ultrasuede, Lutradur, cheesecloth, and more.

- Fabric should be completely dry before transferring. Dampness interferes with the transfer process.

- Protect delicate fabric by using muslin, copy paper, parchment paper, or Silicone Release Paper as a pressing cloth.

- Iron in a circular motion for up to two minutes. You cannot over-iron TAP on fabric.

- Iron until all the polymer has transferred from the paper to the fabric to ensure washability.

Original artwork scanned and TAPped onto fabric

Paper

Most papers will work, though coated and glossy papers may not. Iron for about 7–10 seconds depending on the size. Think vintage book pages, scrapbook paper, watercolor and printmaking paper, painted papers, and more.

Map transferred to paper, then painted

TAP on a spotted brown paper bag

Bits of TAP left over from trimming other images were used to create this impromptu card.

TAP on paper tape

Wood

Use a 1″ piece of low-tack tape to tape one side of the TAP to the wood to keep the TAP from shifting while you are ironing. Do not move the iron too vigorously. Use small, widening circles. The transfer may take only 7–10 seconds, depending on the size.

TAP on wood

Metal and Mica

Use a 1″ piece of low-tack tape to tape one side of the TAP to these nonabsorbent surfaces to keep the TAP from shifting while you are ironing. Place the iron on the TAP and gently iron over the transfer area. Depending on the size, the transfer could take about 4 seconds. Because the surfaces are nonabsorbent, the polymer has nowhere to go and will smear if over-ironed. These surfaces should be thin so that they can be heated evenly and quickly. Craft metals work best. *Important!* The metal will be hot—be prepared with an X-Acto knife, tweezers, or a similar item to lift and peel the edge of the TAP after the transfer.

TAP on brass craft metal

TAP on mica

Glass

TAP transfers to glass are very unpredictable. I consider them on the advanced level. Always test the item or glass before committing to the project. To prevent breakage and cracking, you must start with a cool iron and heat the TAP and glass at the same time. Important! Wear safety goggles in case the glass breaks. Follow the steps for Metal and Mica (page 15).

Various art materials transferred onto white cotton fabric

TAP Lesson

Mixing Media

Mix before TAPping:

- Color over images printed on TAP.
- Paint a background on TAP and then print over it.
- Draw on TAP with a marker, and color with chalk pastels.
- And… (What else can you think of?)

TAP Lesson

Black Ink Creep

Black printer ink has a tendency to smear if over-ironed on surfaces other than fabric. While the transfer is still warm, scrape away or push any stray black ink back into place with an X-Acto knife, cuticle stick, or your fingernail. After it cools, it won't move.

TAP Lesson

"Reusing" TAPped Images

Like what you just TAPped? Scan it, print it, and use it in another project or print it on TAP to TAP again.

TAP Lesson

Make a Sampler

A surface sampler is the best way to learn about, catalog, and showcase your TAP talents.

This book is a sampler of TAP transfers on a variety of surfaces. The photos are still lifes taken in my home on Glade Valley Farm

Lesley
2013

TAP surface sampler book

Sampler cover

Troubleshooting

Lesley Riley's TAP Transfer Artist Paper (by C&T Publishing)
is referred to as TAP throughout the chapter.

TAP should work beautifully every time—on fabric. Applying TAP to other
surfaces requires practice and knowledge of the ins and outs of each surface.
Like any other art technique or tool, TAP requires practice and familiarity for
mastery and success.

That said, following are the factors that can cause problems with TAP.

- **AGE**—TAP has a shelf life of about three years from the packaging date. That includes the time it is on the shelf in a store too, not just in your house. A dry climate can shorten its life too. Do not store TAP in a hot, dry place. If you're comfortable, chances are your TAP is comfortable too.

- **EXPOSURE TO AIR**—TAP is sensitive to dry heat and humidity. Always keep it in a sealed bag before and after printing if you are not transferring it right away. I use a zip-type bag. Depending on your climate, even a day outside of the pack may affect its performance, both before and after printing.

TAP Lesson
Reviving Dry TAP
Artist Liz Kettle lives in dry Colorado. If her TAP isn't transferring as expected, she has found that a fine, light mist of water on the paper will get it going. Hold the paper upright and mist.

- **IRONING**—Ironing must be done on a firm, flat surface. If the iron, TAP, and surface the TAP is being ironed to do not come into complete contact, spotty areas of incomplete transfers can result. Believe me, after all these years of practice, I still have to go back sometimes and iron certain areas again, and sometimes use more pressure. I *always* peel back and check before removing the paper entirely so that I can do just that.

- **PRINTING**—Sometimes I hear from people who unknowingly printed on the wrong, or uncoated, side of the paper. The back of the paper is pale lavender/pink. This is the easiest problem to fix. Just place the TAP back into your printer and print again on the coated white side.

- **SEALANTS AND FINISHES**—Some fabrics and surfaces may have a coating on them, such as waterproofing, antitarnishing, or other coatings. Sizing in fabric may also inhibit the transfer process, whether the sizing is added, as in painter's cloth, or natural, such as sericin in silk. Prepare metal surfaces by cleaning them with alcohol, and fabrics by prewashing in hot water. Or you can also choose to use fabrics as is, like the painter's drop cloth that Lu Peters chose for her quilt, Shear Accident (page 30).

■ **BAD BATCHES**—All that said, sometimes there are bad batches. Imagine a 10'- or 20'-wide roll of paper being spray-coated with the special polymer that makes TAP what it is. It is then dried and cut several times, eventually into sheet size. There are bound to be a few duds. Think of how many times you've received a catalog or newspaper with a printing error, a page that is smeared or faded, or a corner that is uncut or folded. Even quality control at the factory level cannot catch everything. They once had to scrap a whole master roll of TAP! Fortunately this is not common, though. I have printed hundreds of sheets for use in my classes, and never once has anyone had a problem. I have never had a problem either, and I can't begin to count how many sheets I've used.

Anyone who has less-than-perfect results after following the instructions can write to me anytime for troubleshooting. I am always happy to help.

The cure f
anything is
ter, sweat,
or the sea

Karen vo

Stills from a Lif

Love—
TAP Doodles
Art Quilt

Joanne Sharpe

Finished size: 14″ × 12″

Create a garden of individual hand-drawn doodle blossoms on colorful
fabric using TAP Transfer Artist Paper. It's an easy way to use doodle drawings as
design elements in the perfect position on an art quilt.

Materials and Supplies

- TAP*: 1 or more sheets, depending on the size of your quilt
- Black Copic brush-tip marker
- Dye-Na-Flow dyes by Jacquard
- Hand-dyed/hand-painted cotton fabric in the size of your choice
- Backing fabric in a size to match top
- Binding fabric, if desired
- Batting
- Black thread
- Sewing machine

Lesley Riley's TAP Transfer Artist Paper (by C&T Publishing)—referred to as TAP throughout the project

Method

Refer to TAP Transfer Basics (pages 11–17), Troubleshooting (pages 18 and 19), and the TAP packaging as needed.

1. Paint a piece of cotton fabric with paint or inks. The pictured quilt was painted with Dye-Na-Flow paint to create a loose, colorful background.

2. Fill a sheet of TAP with loose flower doodles using a black Copic brush-tip marker. Fill the entire page with drawings. If you are going to use any lettering, be sure to mirror it.

3. Cut out the shapes of the drawings, leaving about ⅛″ outside the black outlines. Transfer the designs to the painted fabric into a pleasing composition.

4. Make a quilt sandwich with the batting and backing fabric, with the painted fabric as the top layer.

5. Add free-motion stitching with black thread around the flower shapes for dimension and texture. Bind as desired.

Run Rabbit Run

ONCE UPON A TIME THERE WAS A
HARE WHO, BOASTING HOW HE
COULD RUN FASTER THAN ANYONE
ELSE, WAS FOREVER TEASING
TORTOISE FOR ITS SLOWNESS.
AESOP

LE LIEVRE.

Lesley Riley
Finished size: 8″ × 10″

I love creating art that tells a story. What better way to play around with kraft•tex's wonderful ability to accept incised text than to stamp a few of Aesop's words to accompany this vintage rabbit image?

Materials and Supplies

- kraft•tex (by C&T Publishing), white: 1 piece cut large enough to frame your image plus an additional area above or below the image for stamping text
- TAP*: 1 sheet printed with your image—mirror the image if the direction matters or if it includes writing
- Metal or rubber alphabet stamps
- Permanent-ink stamp pad
- Stretched canvas (I used an 8″ × 10″ canvas.)
- Fabric to cover canvas
- Staple gun or tacky glue
- Elmer's glue
- Old credit card or similar
- Paint or stain to age kraft•tex (*optional*)

* Lesley Riley's TAP Transfer Artist Paper (by C&T Publishing)—referred to as TAP throughout the project

Method

Refer to TAP Transfer Basics (pages 11–17), Troubleshooting (pages 18 and 19), and the TAP packaging as needed.

1. Plan ahead to allow room for the words you will be stamping and the size of your stamps. Decide on the placement of your text and image, and transfer the image to the kraft•tex.

2. If you want an indented, letterpress-style text, use metal stamps and a hammer on a protected surface such as a cutting mat. You can ink your metal stamps so that the letters you imprint will have the color of your choice. Otherwise, use a rubber stamp alphabet set and permanent stamp ink.

3. When you are finished stamping, stain or age the kraft•tex, if desired.

4. Prepare the display canvas by covering it with fabric that coordinates with your artwork. Cover the blank canvas with a thin layer of Elmer's glue, spreading it evenly with an old credit card. Place your fabric right side down and center the glued side of the canvas on the fabric. Flip over the canvas and smooth the fabric from the center out.

5. Working on the long sides first, pull the fabric firmly around to the back of the canvas and use a staple gun to secure it along the stretcher bars. Repeat on the other side. Do the same on the 2 short sides, mitering the corners as if you were wrapping a package. Staple the fabric in place. If you are using glue to fasten the fabric to the back of the canvas, follow the same steps but secure with glue. See Emma's Journal (page 51) for complete instructions on gluing fabric onto a canvas.

6. Using glue, attach the kraft•tex artwork to the fabric-covered canvas. Cover with a heavy book until glue dries to ensure firm contact.

Lutradur Desk Lamp

Lesley Riley

Finished size: 5″ wide × 8″ high × 5″ deep

I love making lampshades that combine favorite images with translucent fabrics and materials. I chanced upon this super easy lamp kit at my favorite art store and immediately thought—Lutradur! TAP Transfer Artist Paper and Lutradur go together like peanut butter and jelly. (For more information on Lutradur see my book *Fabulous Fabric Art with Lutradur*, from C&T Publishing.)

Materials and Supplies

- Paper Fusion Creative Lamp Kit (I used the 5″ × 8″ lamp frame from Dick Blick.)
- Lutradur: 2 sheets regular weight (70 gm) (from Lutradur Mixed Media Sheets, by C&T Publishing)
- TAP*: 2 sheets printed with your images sized to fit the lamp panel—mirror the image if the direction matters or it includes writing
- Tacky glue, Scotch Quick-Dry Adhesive, or heavy-duty double-stick tape (I used carpet tape.)

Lesley Riley's TAP Transfer Artist Paper (by C&T Publishing)—referred to as TAP throughout the project

Method

Refer to TAP Transfer Basics (pages 11–17), Troubleshooting (pages 18 and 19), and the TAP packaging as needed.

1. Cut out the printed TAP sheets to fit the lamp frame and transfer them to the Lutradur.

2. Using the template in the lamp kit, trim all 4 images to size.

3. Assemble the lamp and the Lutradur panels, following the instructions in the kit.

. . . .

Tip

I used strips of double-sided carpet tape so that I have the option of adding new panels if I ever want to change the look.

. . . .

4. Plug in the lamp, turn it on, and light up your space.

Be Peace Bag

Marie Z. Johansen
Finished size: 8½″ × 7½″

Marie designed this bag as a reminder to keep life in perspective. She took
this image of a former neighbor's Buddha statue in the early 1990s and
has used it many times in her artwork.
This bag was designed as a small everyday purse. It can be worn as a cross-body or
shoulder bag or used as a clutch if you want to eliminate the strap completely. You can
easily make the bag smaller or larger—at the provided pattern size, it will carry the
essentials: wallet, phone, some cosmetics. The amount of weight that the bag can carry
will be somewhat dependent on the material you use to make the strap.

Materials and Supplies

- kraft•tex (by C&T Publishing): 1 package (18″ × 1.63 yards)
- TAP*: 1 sheet printed with original photograph—mirror the image if the direction matters or it includes writing
- COLORHUE dyes, fabric paint, or acrylic inks
- Zipper: 7″–9″
- Sewing machine
- *Optional:*
  Ribbons, yarn, or other material for strap
  Dorland's Wax Medium
  Heat gun or embossing gun

* Lesley Riley's TAP Transfer Artist Paper (by C&T Publishing)—referred to as TAP throughout the project

Method

Refer to TAP Transfer Basics (pages 11–17), Troubleshooting (pages 18 and 19), and the TAP packaging as needed.

Seam allowances are ¼″.

1. Cut a piece of kraft•tex 18″ × 8″ and soak it in very hot water. Using rubber gloves, scrunch it as much as you can to create interesting patterning. Let the kraft•tex dry well. You can smooth it down some, but be careful to preserve the scrunch marks as much as possible.

2. Use COLORHUE dyes, fabric paints, or inks to create patterning on the surface of the kraft•tex. Marie used COLORHUE brown and pumpkin dyes to create the look and feel of aged leather.

3. Transfer your printed TAP image to the surface of the kraft•tex, taking into consideration the seam allowances that will be needed in sewing together the bag.

4. To increase the stability of the dye, as well as to add a bit of water resistance, Marie added a layer of Dorland's Wax Medium and buffed it into the surface until the waxy feeling was gone. Optionally, a light shot with a heat gun blends the image and the wax very well.

5. Fold the kraft•tex in half, right sides together (to a 9″ × 8″ size), and lightly score or otherwise mark the bottom folded edge.

6. Separate the zipper before sewing it in by removing the metal zipper stop. If the zipper is longer than needed, just cut the ends off. If the zipper is the same size as the bag, remove the metal stop with pliers.

7. Pin and sew the zipper to each side of the top of the bag with the right side facing *out* and the zipper lined up with the top edge. Note: The zipper should be long enough so that no further seaming is required on the top. After sewing each zipper side, zip the zipper halfway and hand sew a zipper stop to replace the metal stop that you removed to separate the zipper.

8. Turn the bag inside out so that right sides are together. Sew together the side seams.

9. Finger-press open the side seams. Press the edges of the bag together so that the side seams line up with the bottom fold. This step will square off the bottom of the bag to give it some depth. Draw a line that is about ⅜" from the tip of the corner of the bag and sew along that line; backstitch gently to ensure that the stitching will not pull out. (You can vary the size in this step by moving your stitching line closer to or further away from the edge.) Clip the corners. Repeat on the other side seam.

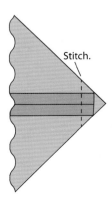

Stitch.

10. Turn the bag right side out—a little patience goes a long way here! Be gentle. When the bag is turned, work the edges of the corners to crispness with a blunt tool such as a larger-sized bamboo knitting needle. Don't use anything too sharp or too pointy or you will poke through the bag.

11. Make a strap using materials of your choice and attach it to the bag.

Shear Accident—
Mini Art Quilt

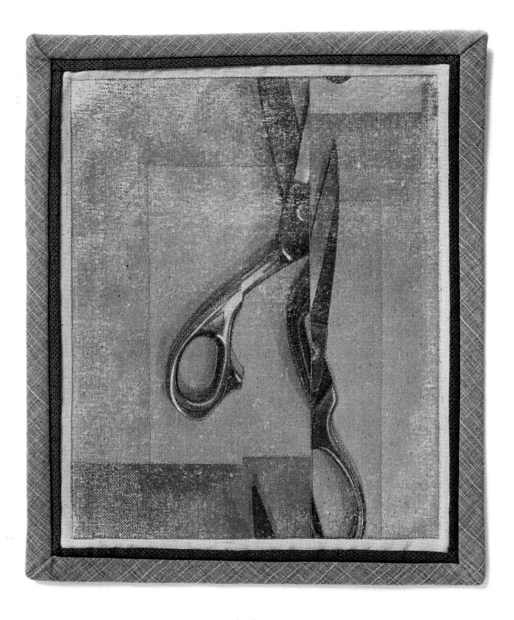

Lu Peters

Finished size: 10¼″ × 13″

Lu has been experimenting with TAP Transfer Artist Paper on highly textured fabrics to achieve depth and aged effects for her transferred photographs. She discovered that the sizing in many fabrics acts as a resist to the polymer on the TAP and can be used to create a variety of interesting patinas and surface effects. Stiff dupioni silk, which has a lot of sericin, and the heavily sized drop cloths used by painters are two fabrics that yield some fascinating results.

Materials and Supplies

- TAP*: printed with original photograph—mirror the image if the direction matters or it includes writing
- Unwashed canvas drop cloth: 1 piece 12″ × 15″
- Backing fabric: 1 piece 12″ × 15″
- Batting: 1 piece 12″ × 15″
- Binding fabric: 1 piece 1½″ × 52″
- Inner border fabric: 1 piece 1½″ × 50″ pressed in half lengthwise (*optional*)
- Variegated cotton quilting threads
- Sewing machine

* Lesley Riley's TAP Transfer Artist Paper (by C&T Publishing)—referred to as TAP throughout the project

Method

Refer to TAP Transfer Basics (pages 11–17), Troubleshooting (pages 18 and 19), and the TAP packaging as needed.

1. Transfer the image onto the unwashed drop cloth, using very high heat and very heavy pressure, keeping the iron moving constantly. This takes much longer than transfers on standard fabrics because of the sizing. Allow about 4–5 minutes, checking frequently to see if the image has transferred to your liking. Remove the TAP paper.

2. Distress the transferred surface with a plastic spoon to scratch off some of the image from the drop cloth and blur the design.

3. After the fabric has cooled, machine quilt as desired.

4. Trim to the finished size (based on the size of your photo), leaving a 1″ frame around the image.

5. Add the inner border (Lu hand-mitered the corners). Then add the binding to create a frame effect.

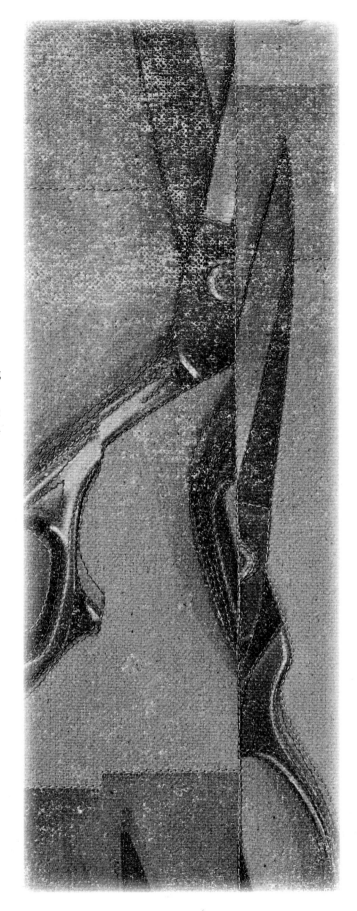

TAP
Doodle Pillow

Lynn Krawczyk

Finished size: 14″ × 14″

Can you ever have too many decorative pillows? Lynn doesn't think so. Pillows are the easiest way to change up the decoration in a room and to also add some of your own personality. But why buy one from a big-box store? Not only are they expensive, but they are also impersonal. It is so much better to create your own design— which is super easy to do with TAP Transfer Artist Paper. Lynn loves doodling directly on the TAP with markers. It lets her be free with the image and it's incredibly fun! This pillow cover is a snap to make and can be customized to fit any decor.

Materials and Supplies

- Fabric: 2 pieces in different colors, each 14½″ × 14½″
- TAP*: 1–2 sheets, depending on your design
- 14″ × 14″ pillow form
- Buttons: 7, size ½″ diameter
- Broad-tipped markers in black, orange, and red
- Perle cotton embroidery thread, size 8
- Embroidery needle
- Sewing machine

* Lesley Riley's TAP Transfer Artist Paper (by C&T Publishing)—referred to as TAP throughout the project

Method

Refer to TAP Transfer Basics (pages 11–17), Troubleshooting (pages 18 and 19), and the TAP packaging as needed.

1. Trace a 3″-diameter circle onto cardboard and cut it out.

2. Using a black marker with a broad tip, trace 7 circles directly onto the TAP.

TAP Lesson

Work on the white side of the TAP, not the colored side. Work gently so as not to scratch the surface coating.

Broad markers are easier to use directly on the TAP—fine-point and medium-point markers can leave gouges. Trace lightly; otherwise you may scratch the TAP.

3. Freehand draw a smaller circle, about ½″ inside the 3″ circle, and make stripes along the inside of the ring, filling in every other stripe solid black.

4. Draw little X's around the inside of the stripe circle.

5. Transfer the TAP circles onto the fabric for the front of the pillow, arranging them as shown in the photograph (page 32).

TAP Lesson

Consider using fabric with some tonal color texture. This adds some interest without competing with the TAP design. The sample for this project uses hand-dyed fabric by Catherine Arnett.

6. After all of the TAP circles are transferred, color in the blank stripes in the circles with the other colored markers.

7. Sew a small button in the center of each TAP circle.

8. Outline the 3 center TAP circles with hand stitching.

9. Pin the pillow front and back fabrics right sides together and sew all the way around, leaving a 9″ opening in the middle of one side.

10. Turn the pillow cover right side out and insert the pillow form.

11. Pin the 9″ opening closed with the edges turned in. Hand stitch the whole side with embroidery thread. Repeat this stitching on the other side to give it some nice detail.

TAP That Journal

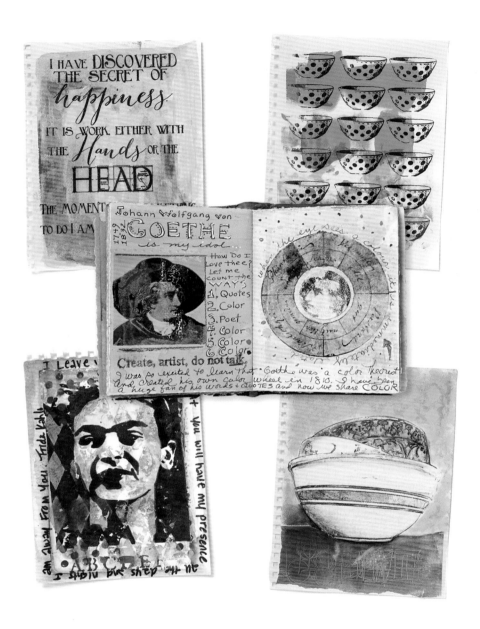

Lesley Riley and Pam Carriker

Finished size: assorted—10″ × 7″ to 9″ × 12″

Using TAP Transfer Artist Paper in your art journal is a wonderful way to record or experiment with ideas and inspiration. We find it a more artful and satisfying approach to gluing a favorite photo or image onto the page. The added bonus is that you can paint, draw, stamp, and write right over the transfer. Oh! And did we mention that you can TAP *over* anything already on the page? The polymer on the TAP will seal charcoal, pastel, oil pastel—all those messy materials that like to smudge and smear.

Materials and Supplies

- Art journal, preferably for mixed media or watercolor
- TAP* printed with your images or artwork—mirror the image if the direction matters or it includes writing
- Assorted art-journaling tools and materials from your stash: paint, inks, stamps, stencils, pens, and so on

Lesley Riley's TAP Transfer Artist Paper (by C&T Publishing)—referred to as TAP throughout the project

Methods

Refer to TAP Transfer Basics (pages 11–17), Troubleshooting (pages 18 and 19), and the TAP packaging as needed.

Art journals are highly personal. Use your creativity and imagination to create your own journal pages. The following is how Pam and I created our pages.

Secret of Happiness

Lesley Riley

I first painted this 9" × 12" journal page with a combination of acrylic inks and craft paint. I typed the quote large enough to fill a full sheet of TAP using a combination of fonts and printed it in reverse on TAP. The quote was then transferred over the painted page.

Bowled Over

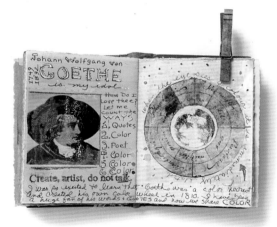

Lesley Riley

I created the colored background on this journal page when I rolled my brayer on the page to clean off excess paint. I was experimenting with repeat patterns and TAPped a full page of bowls onto the journal page.

I ♥ Goethe

Lesley Riley

This is a spread from my handmade journal. The backgrounds were painted with fluid acrylics. The Goethe image, quote, and 1809 color wheel are TAP transfers.

Self Portrait

Pam Carriker

Pam began this journal page by printing some of her lino block carving designs onto TAP. She then used a Gelli plate and stencils to print with acrylics on top of the black design. The black layer will be the top layer of the completed transfer, because the first layer on the TAP paper ends up as the top layer of the transfer. When layering onto TAP, think *first on—last off*.

Finally, Pam added letters with a stencil, placed backward on the TAP so they will be in the correct orientation when transferred. Pam then transferred the TAP into her water-color journal.

Painted Bowls

Lesley Riley

I started with a photograph of three of my favorite bowls. Using Photoshop, I applied the Rubber Stamp filter to the image, basically creating a black-and-white line drawing that I enlarged to fit a sheet of TAP. I trimmed away the excess white areas around the bowls and transferred just the bowls to a blank journal page.

I made the already-transferred TAP paper into a mask by cutting out the shape of the bowls and placing it over the printed bowls. This allowed me to add color to the page with a stencil, acrylic paint, and PanPastel, without getting any color on the bowls themselves. I added texture to the bottom bowl with Golden Crackle Paste. I painted the bowls with acrylics and touches of PanPastel.

I didn't want to leave the bowls floating in air, so I found a leftover scrap of paper, cut a slit underneath the bowl bottom, and slid it up under the bowl. Shadows were added with my favorite "works over anything" Stabilo Aquarelle pencil.

Fiona—A TAP Portrait

Theresa Wells Stifel
Finished size: 11″ × 14″

Theresa loves creating mixed-media collage art. Part of the fun is the hunt for a face to play with. She often looks at old postcards or newspaper ads to scope out the faces. Fiona is based on a fashion ad from a 1967 newspaper.

Materials and Supplies

- Stretched canvas
- Acrylic paint (good quality, not craft paint)
- Ruler
- Pencil
- Paintbrush
- Found papers
- TAP*: 1 sheet printed with found image of a person that includes head and upper torso—mirror the image if the direction matters or it includes writing
- Vintage fabric
- Paper-backed fusible web: 1 piece 8½" × 11"
- Gel medium
- Embroidery floss

Lesley Riley's TAP Transfer Artist Paper (by C&T Publishing)—referred to as TAP throughout the project

Method

Refer to TAP Transfer Basics (pages 11–17), Troubleshooting (pages 18 and 19), and the TAP packaging as needed.

1. Prepare to paint your canvas by penciling in stripes of varying widths on the canvas. Paint the stripes and let the paint dry.

2. Paint random collage papers with acrylic paint for the hair.

3. Transfer the TAP image onto vintage fabric (Theresa used an old tablecloth).

4. Iron the fusible web onto the back of the printed image, remove the paper backing, and cut out the image. The fusible web and polymer on the TAP transfer will allow for good, clean cuts.

5. Place a heavy book or ironing pad under the inner part of the canvas to provide support. Place the image on the canvas, right side up. Cover it with muslin, Silicone Release Paper, or parchment to function as a pressing cloth. Iron to fuse the face/torso to the canvas.

6. Paint in the dress shape over the transferred dress area with acrylic paint.

7. Cut the found, painted papers for hair and apply the papers with gel medium.

8. Paint random polka dots with the end of a paintbrush to balance the composition.

9. When everything is dry, hand embroider the areas you would like to highlight. Theresa satin stitched Fiona's glasses and lips with 3 strands of DMC floss.

10. Don't forget to sign your masterpiece!

Be Careful Where You Tread

Laura LaRue

Finished size: *6″ × 6″*

Like most artistic children, Laura found her first love in drawing. By college she had fallen in love with ceramics. When she was first introduced to encaustics, it was like a bolt of lightning had struck her. Not only could she use any number of found objects and artistic media, but she could also transfer her drawings and add textures as she did with clay. With encaustics and TAP Transfer Artist Paper, Laura can express herself in a way that is totally fulfilling!

Note: This project assumes a basic knowledge in encaustics and/or wax collage. Prepare your encaustic background as desired prior to placing your TAP image in the project. If you are new to encaustics, Laura recommends *Encaustic Workshop* by Patricia Baldwin Seggebruch as an introductory text for this wonderfully addictive art medium.

Materials and Supplies

- TAP*: 1 sheet printed with selected image
- Rigid surface such as Masonite, birch panel, or clayboard
- Encaustic wax medium
- Encaustic paints
- Encaustic palette or griddle
- Metal tins for melting encaustic paints
- Heat gun
- Brushes
- Mark-making tools
- Optional:
    - Oil paints and PanPastel paints
    - Found objects

Lesley Riley's TAP Transfer Artist Paper (by C&T Publishing)—referred to as TAP throughout the project

Method

Refer to TAP Transfer Basics (pages 11–17), Troubleshooting (pages 18 and 19), and the TAP packaging as needed.

1. Cut out the TAP image close to the edge of the print.

2. With the heat gun, warm the wax just slightly in the area where you are going to place the TAP transfer. Be sure that the wax is very smooth and level in that area; otherwise, the image will not entirely transfer onto the wax.

3. Picture side down, place the cut-out TAP image on the warmed wax and rub lightly to make sure it stays in place.

4. Carefully burnish the backside of the TAP with a smooth tool such as a spoon. Be sure to burnish thoroughly, especially the edges. One of the great things about TAP is that you can lift the picture a little to check the transfer and then place it back down if it's not complete.

5. After you peel off the backing paper, you'll notice the clear white of the TAP in areas where there was no color. It was really noticeable in this transfer because it's a simple line drawing and there was no burnishing in the areas where there was no artwork. But never fear! The heat gun will make the white residue transparent.

6. With the heat gun, apply heat carefully to the image transfer. The white areas will turn transparent, revealing whatever colors or details are underneath.

7. The great thing about using TAP in encaustics is that you can put a layer of clear encaustic medium over it and not worry about the image coming off as the wax is wiped over it. Nothing is more frustrating than seeing your carefully transferred image smeared off as it is coated with a layer of wax. With TAP it is really easy to get that first layer of wax over the image without worrying.

Treasure Boxes and Cards

Lesley Riley
Assorted sizes

Artists and creatives are always told to think outside the box. Well, I'm going to turn the tables and say, let's embrace the box. Create a toy, treasure, jewelry, or recipe box. Craft a craft box, a stash for your secret dreams, or a memory box of childhood mementos. There's no need to box in your ideas and inspiration anymore.

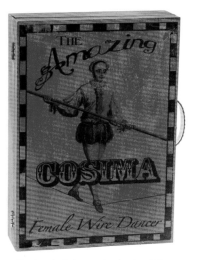

Recipes for a Happy Life by Lesley Riley
Finished size: 6″ × 4″ × 4″

Cosima's Suitcase by Lesley Riley
Finished size: 7″ × 10½″ × 2″

Oh La La by Lesley Riley
Finished size: 4½″ × 6″ × 2″

Treasure Boxes

Materials and Supplies

- Walnut Hollow Basswood Recipe Box
  (Recipes for a Happy Life)
- Walnut Hollow Keepsake Box (Cosima's Suitcase)
- Walnut Hollow Card Box (Oh La La)
- TAP*: the number of sheets will depend on the size of
  your boxes
- Acrylic ink or watered-down acrylic paint
  (I used Liquitex ink.)
- Soft brush
- Low-tack tape
- Optional:
    Wooden discs in 5 graduated sizes plus a button
    plug (from Lara's Crafts)
    Tacky glue for discs
    Antiquing glaze or paints for distressing
    Box hardware (I added a closure and handle to
    Cosima's Suitcase)

* Lesley Riley's TAP Transfer Artist Paper (by C&T Publishing)—
referred to as TAP throughout the project

Method

*Refer to TAP Transfer Basics (pages 11–17), Troubleshooting
(pages 18 and 19), and the TAP packaging as needed.*

1. If you'd like, paint or stain the box exteriors and interiors
in desired color(s). Allow them to dry thoroughly.

2. Measure the box area you will transfer to. Prepare your
text or image so that it fits this area. (I created a new docu-
ment in Photoshop that had the same dimensions as the
box front and arranged my text and images to fit in this area.
After printing in reverse, I cut out the text and image with
their surrounding white area to the same dimensions as the
areas I transferred to so that the TAP paper could easily be
centered and line up perfectly for transferring.)

3. When the box is dry, transfer text and/or images onto
the box top and sides as desired. (I found it helpful to tape
the sides of the box closed when I transferred the text
onto the recipe box front.) Tape the TAP to one side of
the box and iron to transfer. Peel back and check at the
corners to ensure that the transfer is complete before
removing TAP entirely.

4. Distress the box as desired. Add any hardware. For the
recipe box, I decorated the top with a stack of ink-stained
wooden discs, topped with a button plug.

Recipe Cards

Materials and Supplies

Note: A total of 4 photos or 4 quotes (with surrounding white area) will fit on 1 sheet of TAP.

- 3" × 5" ruled index cards
- TAP* printed with 3" × 5" photo images—mirror the image if the direction matters or it includes writing
- TAP (sized for 3" × 5" cards) printed with mirror-image quotations
- Painter's tape
- Scrap paper
- *Optional, depending on your embellishing techniques:*
  - Awl or other sharp-pointed object
  - Rubber stamps
  - Stencils
  - Sequin waste
  - Foam brushes
  - Acrylic paint, spray inks, Glimmer Mist, PanPastel
  - StazOn or other permanent-ink pad
  - Pigment ink pads

* Lesley Riley's TAP Transfer Artist Paper (by C&T Publishing)—referred to as TAP throughout the project

TAP Lesson

Sequin waste makes a fabulous stencil when you need little dots.

Method

Refer to TAP Transfer Basics (pages 11–17), Troubleshooting (pages 18 and 19), and the TAP packaging as needed.

Card Fronts

1. *Optional:* With photos already printed onto TAP, use an awl to scratch in free-form or stenciled designs into preprinted photo backgrounds or details of photos before transferring. Scratched areas will transfer as white.

2. Add visual interest onto card fronts using stencils, paint, or pigment ink stamp pads. You can also use rubber stamps to add details.

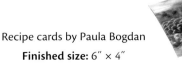

3. Transfer the photo images onto the ruled side of the index cards. Use low-tack painter's tape to hold images in place while transferring.

Card Backs

Let go of what you can't control. Channel all that energy into living fully in the now.
Karen Salmansohn

1. To add color to the back of the index cards, gently paint or add color to create subtle backgrounds using acrylics, pastels, pencils, and so on.

2. If desired, add additional color to the printed TAP page of quotes before transferring using a soft brush of paint or ink, spray inks, stencils, or PanPastel.

TAP Lesson

Paint or spray lightly from a distance above the TAP so that it doesn't get too wet. Immediately blot up excess ink or moisture using scrap paper or a clean cloth. Let the TAP dry briefly before transferring.

3. Transfer the quotations onto the colored backgrounds. Use painter's tape to hold quotes in place while transferring.

4. Add details with rubber stamps, pens, pencils, and so on.

Recipe cards by Paula Bogdan
Finished size: 6" × 4"

Faux Bone Pendants

Sandy Lupton

Assorted sizes

Faux Bone is a nontoxic, flat PVC plastic that can be cut, filed, sanded, carved, drilled, and more to make beautiful, lightweight jewelry. It comes in several thicknesses and is available at www.fauxbone.com. It comes in sheets and precut shapes. Faux Bone basics and tutorials are also available on their website.

Materials and Supplies

- Faux Bone sheets: 1/16" thickness
- 3M sanding block, medium grit
- Jewelry file or fingernail file
- Scanned images of original art or photos
- TAP*: printed with images sized to fit your pendants (1"–3"-wide images are perfect for jewelry)—mirror any images if the direction matters or that include writing
- Sharpie marker
- Mod Podge Matte or Golden Soft Gel medium
- Foam brush
- Burnishing tool (a spoon or any flat, slick object works fine)
- Heavy-duty scissors (for 1/16" Faux Bone sheets)
- Drill
- Jeweler's saw (for thicker Faux Bone)
- Clear acrylic spray
- 2-part epoxy such as ICE Resin
- Bead stringing wire and crimps
- Crimping tool
- Clear acetate for cutting template
- Craft knife
- Acrylic paint in burnt umber (optional)

Lesley Riley's TAP Transfer Artist Paper (by C&T Publishing)—referred to as TAP throughout the project

Additional Materials for Each Necklace

BOAT

- Copper chain (from Michaels)
- 20 gauge copper wire for wrapping
- 16 gauge copper wire for closure
- Round-nose pliers and wire cutters
- Eyelets and eyelet setter
- Sea glass beads
- Copper sheet

SUN/MOON

- Assorted beads
- 16 gauge copper wire
- Round-nose pliers, wire cutters
- Eyelet and eyelet setter
- Copper sheet
- Lampwork beads such as those from www.etsy.com/shop/blackbearart or craft and bead stores

BLUE/RED FLORAL

- Pewter clasp
- Assorted beads
- Screw eye
- ⅛" Faux Bone (thicker than the ¹⁄₁₆" recommended for the other pendants)

CHAIR

LLAMA

- Pewter clasp
- Assorted beads
- Head pin for dangle
- Bezel such as those from
  www.spellbinderspaperarts.com

- Assorted beads
- Silk ribbon
- Bezel such as those from
  www.spellbinderspaperarts.com
- Lampwork beads such as those from
  www.etsy.com/shop/blackbearart
  or craft and bead stores

Method

Refer to TAP Transfer Basics (pages 11–17), Troubleshooting (pages 18 and 19), and the TAP packaging as needed.

1. Faux Bone has a shiny surface, so your first step is to sand it to roughen up the surface. A foam sanding block from the hardware store works well. Sand the entire piece on both sides with a back-and-forth motion and then a circular motion. *Important: Sand it well—this allows the transfers to adhere.*

2. Size down your photographs or images and print them on TAP.

3. Trim the printed image from the TAP sheet and trace the outline onto your Faux Bone sheet—a Sharpie or wax pencil will do the trick. Smear a thin layer of Mod Podge Matte or Golden's Soft Gel medium onto the Faux Bone inside of your outline. Use your finger to avoid brush marks, or use a small foam brush. Be sure to spread the medium evenly all the way to the edges of the outline.

4. Place your image facedown onto the medium-covered Faux Bone. Hold it in place and burnish it down. Let it sit for 10–15 minutes, then slowly remove the paper backing. Depending on the humidity where you live, it may take a little more or less time to cure.

5. When you are happy with your transferred piece, cut it to fit your bezel or finished size. The 1/16″ Faux Bone thickness can be trimmed with heavy-duty scissors or snips. Thicker sizes must be cut with a jeweler's saw or a jigsaw. File and sand the edges smooth. Apply a clear acrylic spray to protect the image and glue it into your bezel with 2-part epoxy. You can also drill your piece and rivet it to a piece of sheet metal or hang it like it is. If you are working with thicker Faux Bone, you can add an eye screw to the top for hanging.

TAP Lesson

If your image did not adhere completely, you can burnish it back down and let it sit for a few more minutes before removing the backing. You can also use a little heat from an iron, but be careful not to let it burn—it only takes a few seconds. If you are unhappy with your transfer, let it cool and then you can sand the image off and start over. Or you can flip it and start again on the back.

Helpful Hints

1. Make a cutting template for your bezel by inking the rim and stamping it onto paper or clear acetate. Trim it and trace it on your Faux Bone sheet for perfect sizing. Remember to trim inside the line; then file and sand your shape until it fits into your bezel.

2. You can enhance your pieces with acrylic paint after you transfer your image. Spray with workable matte fixative and paint, and then top with spray acrylic to protect it.

3. For an antique or vintage look, after you transfer your image, carve or scratch up the edges and rub in burnt umber acrylic paint. Rub off most of the paint, but leave it in the cracks and around the corners. Top with spray acrylic.

4. After you transfer your image, scratch into the surface with a craft knife to add white highlights or details into your transfer. Always top with a coat of spray acrylic sealer.

5. Be patient—as with all transfers, humidity, age of the prints, type of medium, and alignment of the planets all affect the final product. If you are having trouble, do a test sheet, varying the time and medium to see what works best for you. If the medium is still wet after 15 minutes, use less medium on the next one.

Libellus—A Mixed-Media Altered Book

Seth Apter

Finished size: 5½″ × 8½″

Seth has always found handmade artists' books to be compelling. The act of opening the cover and turning the pages creates a collaboration between the artist and the viewer in a way that more traditional art cannot. While the inner pages tell the story, the cover provides a glimpse of the mystery that awaits the viewer inside. As such, for this project Seth decided to focus on the book cover using images and words that will hopefully entice the viewer to open the book and become part of the story.

Materials and Supplies

- Old book cover
- Photograph of your choice
- Copyright-free Latin text image
- TAP*: 1–2 sheets, depending on the size of your book
- Metallic foil
- Watercolor paper: 1 piece 8″ × 10″
- Die-cut machine such as those from www.spellbinderspaperarts.com
- Dies such as those from
- Dies such as those from www.spellbinderspaperarts.com:
    - Nestabilities Decorative Elements, Labels 28
    - Nestabilities A2 Curved Matting Basics B
    - Shapeabilities Mix'd Media Elements
- Alphabet rubber stamp set and rubber stamp ink
- Rub-on letters
- Card stock
- Adhesive
- *Optional:*
    - Found metal strip
    - Gilders Paste in black and patina

* Lesley Riley's TAP Transfer Artist Paper (by C&T Publishing)—referred to as TAP throughout the project

Method

Refer to TAP Transfer Basics (pages 11–17), Troubleshooting (pages 18 and 19), and the TAP packaging as needed.

1. Remove the text pages and spine from an old book and work on the front cover.

2. Using photo-editing software, arrange all the elements to be printed on the TAP—copyright-free Latin text to fit the entire cover (be sure to mirror it) and a photo/image. Then print the TAP sheet.

3. Trim the printed text if needed and transfer it onto the book cover.

4. Cut out the image/photo and iron it onto watercolor paper.

5. To make the frame for the cover, die-cut and emboss a piece of metallic foil. Seth used Spellbinders Nestabilities Decorative Elements Labels 28 dies. If desired, reduce the sheen and age the frame by rubbing the surface with black and patina Gilders Paste.

6. Seth used another die from the same set of Spellbinders dies to die-cut the image on watercolor paper so that it would fit perfectly inside the metallic foil frame.

7. Attach the frame and image to the cover using both adhesive and brads.

8. Cut and emboss 2 pieces of card stock to equal sizes (Seth used Spellbinders Nestabilities A2 Curved Matting Basics B die). Using an alphabet rubber stamp set, stamp the Latin words *libellus foruli* onto one of the pieces of card stock. Use the ink pad to ink the edges to provide more contrast.

9. Overlap the 2 pieces of card stock and adhere them to the bottom of the cover.

10. Cut and emboss 2 more pieces of card stock (Seth used the same die from Spellbinders Shapeabilities Mix'd Media Elements). Trim one of the pieces so it just covers the center portion of the other and adhere them together.

11. Using rub-on letters, add the words *the Records* to the card stock die cut. After inking the edges with a stamp pad, adhere it to the top of the book cover.

12. Optional: Cut a piece of found metal to the length of the book cover and adhere it to the right edge of the book cover.

13. Create a new set of pages to use for the inside of this book as desired. Seth attached his cover to the book spine with hand-rusted nail head brads.

Emma's Journal

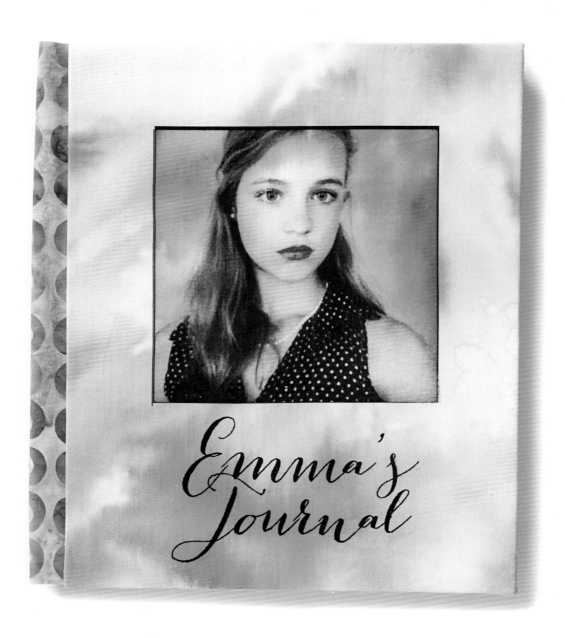

Lesley Riley

Finished size: 8″ × 10″

I created this journal for my oldest granddaughter using my signature expanding journal construction method. Emma is fast approaching sixteen and excels in brains, beauty, athletics, and the art of photography. The photo is one in a series of selfies she took. If I didn't know better, I would have sworn it was done on a professional model shoot.

Hey, I'm the grandmother...

Materials and Supplies

- TAP*: 1 sheet printed with selected image and/or text—mirror the image if the direction matters or it includes writing; cut to 8″ × 10″
- Canvas board: 4 panels 8″ × 10″
- White cotton fabric: 1 fat quarter (18″ × 22″) to paint for the book cover (If you prefer you can use a hand-dyed or commercial fabric.)
- Coordinating fabric: 3 pieces 10″ × 12″ for the back and inside covers
- Binding fabric: 1 piece at least 6″ × 11″ (This can be coordinating fabric or the same fabric as one of the covers. Note: The wider the binding, the more pages you can place in the journal over time.)
- Low-loft batting: 1 piece 8″ × 10″
- Elmer's glue or similar white glue
- Ribbon: 2 yards cut into 1 yard pieces
- Fluid acrylics, acrylic inks, or fabric paint
- Paintbrush
- 90 lb. watercolor paper: up to 3 pieces 22″ × 30″ (Each sheet will provide 9 journal pages; use more sheets if you like.)

* Lesley Riley's TAP Transfer Artist Paper (by C&T Publishing)—referred to as TAP throughout the project

Method

Refer to TAP Transfer Basics (pages 11–17), Troubleshooting (pages 18 and 19), and the TAP packaging as needed.

Prepare Panels

1. Using the paints or inks of your choice, add color to the fat quarter of white fabric. Use a light wash and keep some areas pale or white. Remember that this background color will show through your TAP transfer. Also remember that it will dry lighter. Note: Painting the fabric is optional; you can skip this step and use a hand-dyed or commercial fabric.

2. After the fabric has dried, look for a good spot to place your transfer. Keep in mind that it will need to be centered on a 10″ × 12″ section of the fabric. I hold the fabric and transfer up to a window to see where to best position it prior to transferring.

3. After you have selected the best area for your image, transfer the image to the fabric and trim the fabric to 10″ × 12″.

4. To cover the front panel for the journal, put a thin layer of glue on the front of the canvas panel and place the batting on the panel. (Alternatively, you can stitch or quilt the cover with the batting and then lightly glue the batting in place.) Center the image on the cover fabric over the batting and place it fabric side down on the work surface. The back of the canvas panel will now be facing you.

5. Apply glue to each long side of the canvas panel. Spread it toward the center to cover up to 1" from the edges. Glue one side of the fabric down. Check to confirm that your image is still centered and then glue down the other side.

6. Measure ¼" away from the canvas board corner and clip all 4 corners at a 45° angle.

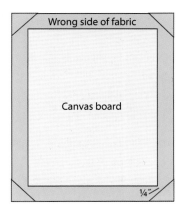

7. Add glue from edge to edge to one of the remaining unglued panels. Working on one corner at a time, fold the outer edge of the fabric toward the center, tuck (or as I like to say, scooch)

the trimmed corner fabric and then fold the edges over and glue into place (like you are wrapping a package!). Repeat on the other 3 corners.

8. To cover the 3 remaining canvas panels, apply a thin layer of glue to the entire panel front. I like to use an old credit card to spread it evenly. If you see the milky white of the glue on the panel, you have too much glue. Hold the panel so that it reflects light to see if you have covered all areas. Any areas without glue will cause a pucker in the finished fabric cover.

9. Place the fabric for the panel right side down. Place the glued side of the panel in the center of the fabric and press evenly. Flip the panel over and, working from the center outward, smooth the fabric on the panel. Follow Steps 5–7 to finish each panel.

Journal Assembly

1. To create the journal binding, place the 6" × 11" fabric piece right side down. Fold ½" of each short end toward the wrong side of the fabric. Iron it in place. Fold the strip lengthwise. Iron and set aside.

2. Place the front and back covers right side down and side by side with the front cover on the left. Allow 1" or more space between them, depending on the desired finished width of your binding strip.

3. Spread glue on the entire exposed side of the back cover, especially on the edges. You want a good amount of glue, but not so much that it will squeeze out when you place the top board on it.

4. Place ½" of the long raw edge of the binding along the left side of the back cover board. Finger-press in place. Center and place the pieces of ribbon vertically and horizontally. Be careful not to get glue on the ribbon ends!

5. Add glue to the wrong side of the panel you selected as the inside back cover. No need to spread evenly, but do take care to get it along the edges. Place the inside cover board right side up on the back cover, ensuring that it is even and that the binding fabric is placed and secured evenly along the left edges and the ribbons are centered and straight.

6. Repeat Steps 3–5 for the front and inside front cover, omitting the ribbon and being sure that the left side of the binding is straight, secure, and enclosed between the 2 panels.

7. Tear the watercolor paper into 10" × approximately 7⅜" sheets. The width of each sheet should be between 7" and 8". Uniformity of width is not necessary. Stack your sheets and place them on the inside back cover. Tie the ribbons to hold the sheets in place.

Photo Frames

Lesley Riley

Assorted sizes

In a family as large as mine, photos abound, but they rarely make it off the computer or smartphone. Creating a frame that adds another element to a photo or expands on the adage that "every picture tells a story" is the perfect incentive to print, display, and share all those photos you've taken.

Materials and Supplies

- Unfinished wood frames from the craft store, such as Michaels' laser-cut frame and Michaels' Art Minds square frame
- Acrylic ink
- Foam brush
- Designs or images to transfer to the frame
- TAP*: 1–2 sheets per frame depending on the size of the frame

Lesley Riley's TAP Transfer Artist Paper (by C&T Publishing)—referred to as TAP throughout the project

Method

Refer to TAP Transfer Basics (pages 11–17), Troubleshooting (pages 18 and 19), and the TAP packaging as needed.

1. Lightly sand the frame. If desired tint it with acrylic ink or watered-down fluid acrylic. The laser-cut frame was left unfinished. Liquitex ink in yellow medium azo was used for the square frame. Let any paint or ink dry.

2. Select and print the designs or images onto TAP. If the frame is larger than the TAP sheet, refer to Off the Page—Transferring Larger Images (page 62).

3. Tape the TAP to one edge of the frame to hold it in place and iron to transfer.

4. Insert your photo or artwork and enjoy!

You Are My Sunshine by Lesley Riley
Finished size: 8″ × 8″

A Big Hello by Lesley Riley
Finished size: 12″ × 9″

On the Farm—A Shabby Chic Tiled Painting

Lesley Riley

Finished size: 12″ × 12″

I often tell people that I feel like I live in a painting. The farm landscapes that are now a part of my every day always inspire and never cease to amaze me. I wanted to create something more than a photo to remember them by.

Materials and Supplies

- TAP*: 2 sheets
- White mini canvas panels: 9 at 4″ × 4″
- Prepainted black canvas: 12″ × 12″
- Photo, enlarged and sized to fit the 12″ × 12″ square format (Instagram photos are ideal for this project!)
- Elmer's glue or similar
- Sandpaper
- *Optional:*
    Paint and brush to color the canvas
    Distress paint or medium

* Lesley Riley's TAP Transfer Artist Paper (by C&T Publishing)—referred to as TAP throughout the project

Method

Refer to TAP Transfer Basics (pages 11–17), Troubleshooting (pages 18 and 19), and the TAP packaging as needed.

1. Sand each canvas board a bit to create a more absorbent surface.

2. If you want a colored background canvas (color may peek through the edges of the tiles), paint your 12″ × 12″ canvas and the outsides edges now.

3. Using a photo-editing program, such as Photoshop Elements, size your image to 12″ × 12″ at a good print quality resolution (300 dpi). I added a Paintbrush filter to the image to give it a soft painterly feel and mirrored it for printing.

4. To divide the image into 4 sections, use the Cut and Paste functions to place the sections as follows: section 1 on one sheet, sections 2 and 3 on a second sheet, and section 4 on a third sheet.

5. Print each page and cut each section into 4″ × 4″ squares.

6. Transfer each square onto a 4″ × 4″ canvas board. If your image is such that it will be hard to tell which panel goes where or which side is up, do a little prep work by arranging the squares in the correct order (remember—they are reversed, so your squares will be backward at this point). Assign a board to each square and make notations on the back of the board to help you in assembling them on the larger canvas before you transfer.

7. Manually distress the tiles or tile edges if desired. I sanded a few of the corners on the outer tile edges. Do not add any paint or medium type of distress at this time.

8. Align the 9 transferred tiles in proper order next to your canvas. Apply a generous amount of glue to the canvas top and spread evenly. It should be tacky wet but not overly wet at this point. Starting in the upper left corner, apply glue to the back of the first tile and place on the canvas, lining it up with the canvas corners. Continue gluing the tiles across the top row. Glue the second and third rows. When they are all in place, make any minor adjustments you might need to line up the spaces.

9. Distress the finished canvas as desired.

Mixed-Media
Art Card Quartet

Lesley Riley

Assorted sizes

I've been making cards for as long as I can remember, first with construction paper and crayons, and now with a variety of surfaces that take card making to a new level. I consider my mixed-media cards to be mini works of art. In many cases, no additional gift is necessary.

Materials and Supplies

- Strathmore Mixed Media Blank Cards or 90 lb. watercolor paper
- Dick Blick shaped stationery blank
- Frame card: from Carol Doak's Keepsake Frame Cards (from C&T Publishing)
- kraft•tex (from C&T Publishing): cut to desired size of card
- TAP*: printed with photos or other images—mirror the image if the direction matters or it includes writing
- Optional additional images printed on the paper of your choice (I used a vintage image from Antique Graphique's Etsy shop.)
- Micro Pigma pen
- Glitter (I used German glass glitter.)
- Elmer's glue
- Diamond Glaze dimensional adhesive (*optional*)

* Lesley Riley's TAP Transfer Artist Paper (by C&T Publishing)—referred to as TAP throughout the project

Methods

Refer to TAP Transfer Basics (pages 11–17), Troubleshooting (pages 18 and 19), and the TAP packaging as needed.

Hello Baby!

For this style of card, size your desired image so that the main areas will be prominent and fit onto the shaped card. This Dick Blick card has a diameter of 4″, so I printed my photo at 4″ × 4″. Do not trim the TAP image before transferring. Place scrap paper under the card surface to accept the excess transfer inks. Iron to transfer.

Feeling Chipper

For this type of card, size your image to fit the card and iron to transfer. I used kraft•tex and cut it 5½″ × 11″ to create this 5½″ square card. Add text as you choose. In this example, the card was stamped with metal stamps and highlighted with a fine Micro Pigma pen.

Reindeer

Tiny Dancers

In this example, I transferred a photo of my first snowfall here on the farm to a 5″ × 7″ Strathmore Mixed Media card. After ironing a few seconds, I checked to see if the transfer was complete. Then I sprinkled glitter on the upper half of the card, replaced the TAP paper over it, and ironed a bit more to adhere the glitter in the TAP polymer.

You cannot put the glitter down first as it acts as a resist to getting all areas of the image transferred.

I selected a vintage image of a deer for the focal point of the card, printed on bright white copy paper. To give the paper stability for fussy cutting and a glossy, somewhat dimensional gleam to make the image pop, I covered the image with Diamond Glaze dimensional adhesive before cutting it out. The cut image was glued to the card with Elmer's glue.

A card can be a gift, but a card with a photo is one that will surely be cherished. When creating this card, I didn't want the large areas of the frame to compete with the smaller image area. I searched for a copyright-free pattern that I could use to enhance and embellish on the story that the photo was telling. Using Photoshop, I scaled and sized the pattern I found so as not to overwhelm the photo.

I printed the pattern image the same size as the card front (5″ × 7″), cut it out, and transferred the pattern to the card front. If you want the center portion to remain blank, insert a piece of scrap paper inside the card opening to mask that area.

Ideas & Inspiration: Further Ideas to Explore

Lesley Riley's TAP Transfer Artist Paper (by C&T Publishing) is referred to as TAP throughout the chapter.

Off the Page—Transferring Larger Images

I am often asked, "How do you transfer an image that is larger than the TAP paper size?" Depending on your printer, your software, and your familiarity with both, you have several options.

Tiling

First, check to see if your printer driver has an option for Poster Printing. This will allow you to take a large image and print it across two, four, six, or more sheets.

Tiling an image can be done with software programs such as Adobe Photoshop or Illustrator and Windows Paint.

TILING USING WINDOWS PAINT PROGRAM

1. Using Windows Paint, open the image you'd like to print.

2. Select: Print > Page Setup (Vista and Windows 7) or File > Page Setup (in XP).

3. Under Scaling, select Fit To and change the setting to something like 2 × 2 pages for a final transferred image size of 16″ × 21″, or 3 × 4 pages for a final transferred image size of 24″ × 42″. (However, these sizes depend on each user's original image size.)

4. Click OK.

5. Print the image from Paint, making sure to select All Pages.

(Courtesy of www.scottiestech.info)

For Mac users, you can also tile in PosteRazor (free), Tiler, or SplitPrint (last two from the Mac App store for $5–$6). Note the operating system and read the specs; Tiler is for OS 10.7 and up.

Crop and Print

I know that tiling is easier, but I seldom take the time to do it unless I need a really large image. I always use the crop and print method for smaller projects when I need to span only an extra sheet or two of TAP. I have described it thoroughly in On the Farm (page 56).

Lighten Up a Dark Surface

The second-most-asked question I get is, "Is there a TAP for dark fabrics?" Sadly, the answer is no, but hopefully I can also say, not yet. Printer inks are transparent. Some transfer papers have a rubbery/plastic sheet that is printed on, and then that sheet is adhered to a fabric with an iron. TAP fuses directly into and becomes a part of the fabric and other absorbent surfaces. Transfer paper for dark fabrics works with that intermediary paper method as well. If and when the TAP manufacturers figure it out, you'll be among the first to know.

In the meantime, if you want to transfer onto a dark background, you will lose a lot of color and contrast in your image—and that may be just fine for some projects. If you want to integrate an image onto a dark surface without appliquéing or otherwise adhering it to the dark surface, I recommend lightening the surface.

I have successfully used gesso and white fluid acrylic to lay down a white background prior to transferring my images onto dark fabric. If you are working with an image with straight edges and are really precise and careful, you can paint the exact area where the transfer will go so that it will appear seamless. Let the paint dry before you transfer. (I left my paint edges showing for illustrative purposes.)

Another method is to use a white oil pastel to color/add a layer of white over the printed image before ironing. I've tried several art materials (chalk, pastel, rubber-stamp ink, and yes, paint that sticks like glue when ironed). Crayola Portfolio oil pastels seem to best do the trick.

Fabric painted with gesso

Fabric painted with golden titanium white fluid acrylic

White Crayola Portfolio oil pastel layered over printed TAP image prior to transfer

Paint by *Your* Numbers

A line drawing "photo" taken with the Paper Camera app

Not everyone feels comfortable painting or drawing on their own. A great use of TAP is to use your own photo or copyright-free images as an underpainting—on a canvas, in your journal, on fabric, and more.

There are two ways to do this:

■ Turn a photo into a line drawing using a filter in photo-editing software such as Photoshop Elements or a smartphone app such as Paper Camera and add color or paint as desired (see Painted Bowls in TAP That Journal, page 36).

■ You can also transfer the photo as is, or a lightened version of it, and use it as a base for your painting. Remember, there's no need to really stay in the lines like a paint-by-number project. Use your image as a guide and create your own version of the image.

Transferred underpainting ready for the paintbrush

Crease, Crinkle, Fold & Distress

Age your photos before transferring them by adding those bends and creases that are the signs of age on vintage photos and snapshots. Bending and manipulating the printed image prior to transfer will cause some of the coating to flake away from the TAP: No coating, no transfer.

Your distressing can be as simple as bending back a corner of the TAP to as heavy-duty as crumpling the entire photo. Additional distress can be added by scratching into the surface and scraping away some areas, especially around the photo edge.

TAP Lesson

It's important that you brush away any of the coating crumbs from the paper before doing the transfer; otherwise, they will transfer as random spots. On second thought … that might be a good thing.

Alternatively, you can also add color, spots, or stains to the photo with any soft art material that will not scratch the paper coating prior to transferring.

Artful Sachet Bags

Thalia Newton

Thalia scans her original watercolor paintings and transfers them to white taffeta sachet bags. She custom makes the handles with coordinated beads and ties and fills a sheer interior bag with dried lavender enhanced with lavender oil. I wish you could smell them!

Family Recipe

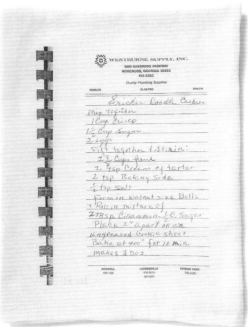

C. Renee Cowart

What a wonderful way to make use of Granny Cowart's treasured hand-written family recipe for snickerdoodles—transfer it onto a flour sack towel that you can use while baking them!

Celebration Dress

Sisters Mary Ellen and Susan, along with their mom, Thelma, created this festive memory dress to celebrate their baby sister's 50th birthday. A collection of words and phrases that define their sister, Chris, were TAP transferred onto a rainbow of 75+ ribbons to create the skirt.

Mary Ellen Kundrat, Thelma M. Macaluso, and Susan Rubinow

I ♥ Horses

Lesley Riley

Although I never dreamed we would be living on a thoroughbred horse farm, I have collected horse memorabilia, paintings, and prints for more than 40 years. Now that I have equine photo ops literally standing at the ready, I can really get creative. Cork makes an excellent background for TAP transfers and is readily available at the craft store in scrapbook paper sheets and smaller adhesive Corkstock Tiles from Canvas Corp.

TAP That Home Decor

Lesley Riley

Canvas and burlap home decor items printed with vintage text and illustrations are *hot* and can fetch upwards of $60 at stores. With TAP and a few Etsy vintage images sources (see Resources, page 69), you can easily create your own for much, *much* less.

If you don't sew, don't despair. You can still do this. Pillow, placemat, napkin, table runners, and more canvas blanks are available from Canvas Corp and other sources.

Mixed-Media Book Cover

Lesley Riley

Who doesn't love to mix media? This book cover was created by TAPping an image onto a Ranger adhesive foil sheet. The image was outlined with Ranger alcohol ink (ginger) and smudged a bit. The word *nature* was stamped into the foil with metal stamps. The entire sheet was adhered to an antique book cover that had raised embossing. The metal was burnished into the embossing to add dimension and texture.

Resources

BASIC SUPPLIES

Most of the supplies used in the projects can be found at quilt or fabric shops, arts and crafts stores, art supply stores, and hardware stores, both local and online.

SPECIALTY PRODUCTS

Lesley Riley's TAP Transfer Artist Paper
Quilt and craft stores
www.ctpub.com

Burlap/Canvas Blanks
Craft stores
www.canvascorp.com

Digital Downloads
www.etsy.com/shop/antiquegraphique
   (Mention this book and receive ten
   free downloads.)
www.etsy.com/shop/graphique
www.etsy.com/shop/madamebricolage

Faux Bone
www.fauxbone.com

Jewelry Supplies and Metal Stamps
Craft or bead stores
www.riogrande.com

kraft•tex
Quilt and craft stores
www.ctpub.com

Lutradur
Quilt and craft stores
www.ctpub.com

Mica
www.volcanoarts.com

Paper Fusion Lamp Kits
www.dickblick.com
www.gpcpapers.com

Crayola Portfolio Oil Pastels
Children's art supply section in arts and crafts stores
www.crayola.com
www.staples.com

Rayon Ribbon
Fabric stores
www.etsy.com/shop/ribbonsmyth

Spellbinders Bezels and Dies
Craft stores
www.spellbinderspaperarts.com

Walnut Hollow Wood Products
Craft stores
www.walnuthollow.com

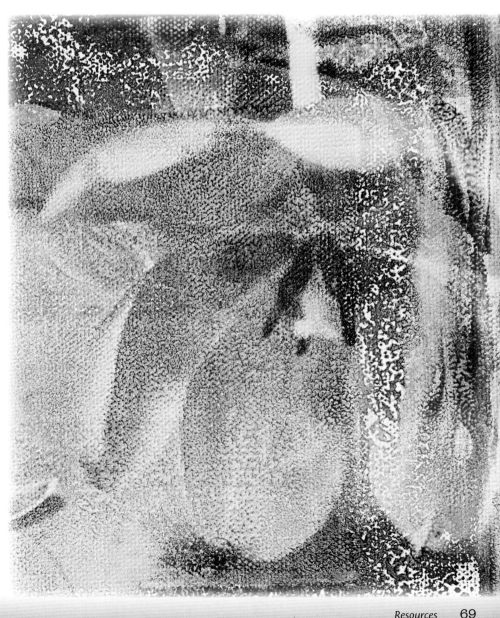

Contributing Artists

Seth Apter • New York, NY
www.thealteredpage.blogspot.com

Paula Bogdan • Springfield, VA
www.littlescrapsofmagic.typepad.com

Pam Carriker • Mansfield, TX
www.pamcarriker.com

Renee Cowart • Buford, GA

Marie Z. Johansen • Friday Harbor, WA
www.musingcrowdesigns.com

Lynn Krawczyk • Plymouth, MI
www.smudgedtextilesstudio.com

Mary Ellen Kundrat,
Thelma Macaluso, and Susan Rubino
Great Neck, NY

Laura LaRue • Crystal Lake, IL
www.lauralarue.weebly.com

Sandy Lupton • Courtland, VA
www.shooting-star-gallery.com
Artists Sandy Lupton

Thalia Newton • Shalimar, FL

Lu Peters • Dallas, TX
www.lupeters.com

Joanne Sharpe • Rochester, NY
www.joannezsharpe.blogspot.com

Theresa Wells Stifel • Falls Church, VA
www.stifelandcapra.com

About the Author

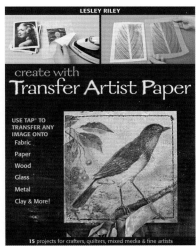

Lesley Riley wears many hats. She is an internationally known mixed-media artist, quilter, teacher, writer, and Artist Success coach/mentor who turned her initial passion for photos, color, and the written word into a dream occupassion. Her art and articles have appeared in numerous publications and juried shows. A former contributing editor of *Cloth Paper Scissors*, Lesley showcased new talent in mixed-media art. Her first book, *Quilted Memories*, brought new ideas and techniques to quilting and preserving memories. Her second book, *Fabric Memory Books*, combined fabric and innovative ideas with the art of bookmaking. Two more books, *Fabulous Fabric Art with Lutradur* and *Create with Transfer Artist Paper*, introduced versatile new materials to the mixed-media art world.

In Lesley's ongoing effort to find the best ways for quilters and mixed-media artists to get permanent imagery on fabric, she introduced Lesley Riley's TAP Transfer Artist Paper—the state-of-the-art technology for iron-on transfers to fabric and other surfaces. The Craft and Hobby Association named it the CHA Innovation Award Winner in winter 2011.

Her passion and desire to help every artist reach her or his creative dreams and potential has led to a growing specialty as an Artist Success expert and coach, providing solutions for artists of all levels. For more information, please visit www.lesleyriley.com.

Great Products

from C&T PUBLISHING

Available at your local retailer or **www.ctpub.com** *or* **800-284-1114**

For a list of other fine books from C&T Publishing, visit our website to view our catalog online.

C&T PUBLISHING, INC.

P.O. Box 1456
Lafayette, CA 94549
800-284-1114

Email: ctinfo@ctpub.com
Website: www.ctpub.com

C&T Publishing's professional photography services are now available to the public. Visit us at www.ctmediaservices.com.

Tips and Techniques can be found at www.ctpub.com > Consumer Resources > Quiltmaking Basics: Tips & Techniques for Quiltmaking & More

For quilting supplies:

COTTON PATCH

1025 Brown Ave.
Lafayette, CA 94549
Store: 925-284-1177
Mail order: 925-283-7883

Email: CottonPa@aol.com
Website: www.quiltusa.com

Note: Fabrics shown may not be currently available, as fabric manufacturers keep most fabrics in print for only a short time.